YOUR KNOWLEDGE HAS VALUE

Bibliographic information published by the German National Library:

The German National Library lists this publication in the National Bibliography; detailed bibliographic data are available on the Internet at http://dnb.dnb.de .

Imprint:

Copyright © 2016 GRIN Verlag, Open Publishing GmbH
Print and binding: Books on Demand GmbH, Norderstedt Germany
ISBN: 9783668561045

This book at GRIN:

http://www.grin.com/en/e-book/378353/leadership-style-and-communication-the-example-of-larry-page

Pascal Pfähler

Leadership Style and Communication. The Example of Larry Page

GRIN Publishing

Larry Page - Leadership style

Pascal Pfähler

A research paper submitted to the University of Applied Management Studies in
fulfilment of the requirements for a course work on Leadership

Date: 22.03.2016

Introduction

The success of any organization depends on the qualities of the leader, his leadership style, and the way he communicates his aims and visions to his employees. At first, it is important to distinguish a leader from a manager, because often both words will be equalized. The most important difference between a leader and a manager is the way they motivate and inspire their teams to achieve prescribed aims. If you consider a manager, you will recognize that his main tasks are organizing, planning and controlling procedures. In contrast to this, a leader sees his tasks in inspiring employees with his visions and motivating them, as much as possible. The idea behind the leadership style is to create creativity, innovation, meaningfulness and change (cf. Educational-Business-Articles, 2016).

This paper intends to show, some theoretical fundamentals about leadership and communication, which will be illustrated through my chosen example "Larry Page". The idea of this paper is also, to connect theoretical knowledge about leadership and communication, with Larry Page´s understanding of leadership.

At the beginning you will get some general information about his private- and working life. Afterwards I will explain different styles of leadership, which I will compare with Larry´s leadership style. At this point it is necessary, to examine whether his philosophy and personality goes with one of the named leadership styles, or not. The third point in my paper describes the synergy of leadership and teams. Leadership creates different ways to lead, recruit, and motivate a team. In addition, it establishes several possibilities to communicate with a team in a special way. Subsequently, I will examine which principles Larry Page has to lead a team successfully. Furthermore, his strengths as well as his weaknesses will be described. The last point of this paper is the interaction of communication and leadership. For every good leader it is necessary to communicate his visions and aims to his team. Larry Page is one of the best examples to underline this hypothesis, because without communication he cannot convey his ideas to the team. In my conclusion I will summarize the general facts of this paper and judge where are similarities and differences between the theoretical leadership style and the one of Page.

General information about Larry Page

Lawrence Edward Page was born on March 26, 1973, in East Lansing, Michigan. "His father, Dr. Carl Victor Page, was a professor of computer science and artificial intelligence at Michigan State University, where Lawrence´s mother, Gloria, also taught computer programming" (Academy of Achievement, 2015).

After his Bachelor of Science degree in engineering at Michigan University, he decided to study computer engineering at Stanford University. There he met Sergey Brin.
After many projects together, they licensed Google.com in 1997. One year later, they founded "Google", as a privately held company, where Page took the position of the CEO and Brin as its president. In 2001, Page and Brin decided to appoint Eric Schmidt as CEO of "Google", while Page took the position of president for products, and Sergey Brin as president for technology. In the following years the success of Google increased dramatically through an excellent Management of the three executives. Beside his success with Google, he had a long relationship with Marissa Mayer, which failed yet. On 8 December 2007 he married Lucy Southworth, a doctoral candidate in Stanford. Together they have two sons. Despite his success with Google, he has to deal with Hashimoto, an autoimmune disease. This illness maybe changed his life, but not his status as a leader (cf. Academy of Achievement, 2015).

Different styles of leadership

Today, there are existing many different styles of leadership. The question which style is the best for leading an organization or a team depends on several terms. As a leader you have to know the personality of your employees. Otherwise you cannot achieve prescribed aims. "In 1938, psychologists Lewin, Lippitt, and White set out to classify and study different types of leadership. Through this study they identified three different leadership styles: autocratic, democratic, and laissez-faire" (JENSEN, L. 2013).

At first I want to explain the autocratic leadership style. "[...] [It] is one in which a single person takes control and makes decisions, directing others in his or her chosen course of action" (MARTIN, M. 2015). Normally an autocratic leader makes all essential decisions, which have a high priority for the company. Individuals do not often work well under autocratic leaders, because they want to be involved in the decision making of the leader. "People who prefer working [...] [...] with strict procedures, checks and balances work well with autocratic leaders" (GILL, E. 2014b). There are many advantages and disadvantages of this leadership style. At the end the success of this and all other styles depends on the industry and the

3

personality of the employees. (cf. GILL, E. 2014b) The next one I want to explain is the democratic leadership style. John Gastil, a professor, who is specialized in communication arts and political science, has written a definition about this leadership style. For him, the democratic leadership style is "Distributing responsibility among the membership, empowering group members, and aiding the group's decision-making process" (GASTIL, J. 1994). The characteristic of this leadership style is the inclusion of employees in decision-making (cf. GILL, E. 2014c). In companies like Google, Apple or Amazon you can see how successful the proper leadership style can be. In this case, the leader of these companies mostly uses the democratic leadership style. Democratic leader have to be team orientated, fair minded and role models. For smart and talented people, this leadership style is the best way to work successfully (cf. GILL, E. 2014c). The laissez-faire leadership style is the last one I want to mention in this topic. This style of leadership allows the employees free decision-making. The leader confers his team individual independence, through his hands-off leadership style. The idea behind this style is to build a strong team with special personalities and abilities. This way of leading is very risky, because it is not the task of a team to make strategic decisions, but rather of the leader. The requirements for a successfully laissez-faire style are well educated-, motivated-, and experienced staff (cf. GILL, E. 2014a).

Classification of Larry Page´s leadership style

In the theoretical part I explained, that the personality of your team is important to know, for choosing the proper leadership style. Also crucial is the philosophy of yourself. When I have to describe the philosophy of Larry Page, I would summarize it with just one quote. In 2013 he said: "We should be building great things that don't exist "(Larry Page, 2013). This sentence does not only illustrate, why Google is so successful. It exhibits a closed community, where all employees have their share of success. Larry Page is known for his unique innovative thinking. But he also knows that he cannot create special things, without his team. That´s why he is searching for smart and talented people, who want to be a part of the big family. He is not an autocratic leader, who uses procedures, checks and balances to lead his team. For him it is important to work with his team in harmony (cf. Akinyemi, S. 2014, p.3 ff.). Beside his quality to recruit the best applicants for implementing his vision and mission, he can motivate and communicate like no one else. His leadership style is based on these three pillars. Without any of these three pillars, the success of Larry Page and his leadership style is endangered. Of course there are arising high costs through his intensive communication with the team, but the relationship with his team is for him the basic module of his work. There are many more

4

things, which Page is enabling his employees, like free meals, medical services or free time for family. These points should make the job of every Google employee more familiar and easier. The result is a higher productivity and a nice atmosphere, in which all employees can work together, for a common aim. This aim will be transmitted by Larry Page. His leadership style is in this point completely different against the laissez-faire style. The employees take an important role in his idea of leading; nevertheless he makes the strategic decisions, which he communicates to his team. Finally, there is only one leadership style left, which can be matched with the one of Page. Sure, there is not one leadership style which describes the one of Page completely, but between his style and the democratic one is a high conformity. Page is team orientated, fair to his employees, and a role model. The fact that he treats every employee on the same way is also an indication for the democratic leadership style.

Leading a team successfully

If you want to build or lead a team successfully, you need passion. Moreover you have to create the right environment for leadership. In the military, the team members develop such selflessness, that they always will do what the senior leader says. But leadership is more than authority. A true leader motivates, communicates, and gives his team a familiar feeling. A team just can work, if all members work together for one common goal. It is the task of the leader to make them feel safe. If the team feels this support, they can achieve every aim of the company (cf. Gleeson, 2015).

If there is a tie between the leader and the team you can define the objectives and the aims of the company. Furthermore you can explain the measures, on which the success is based. In this step it is important not just saying it but rather communicating it correctly to the team. It is not enough to explain objectives, aims and measures one time. You have to support and lead your team members on their way achieving the common aim. Another task of a leader is to recruit the right people for the company projects. It is not possible to only recruit "A" players. Obviously you need some, but you also need some other members. A leader cannot expect to only work with experts. In this case his leadership qualities would not be needed (cf. Pierce, 2013).

Many companies have their own application system and individual requirements. On this way, the can search for the perfect member. Besides the recruitment of members, a leader has to detect strengths and weaknesses of every single member. After this he has to deal with the clearance of weaknesses and the improvement of strengths (cf. Pierce, 2013).

There are much more qualities you need to be a good leader. You have to be a good listener, who is interested in problems of single team members. Moreover you should be sensitive and respectful against them (cf. Olson, 2014). In general, the behavior of a leader should be an example for his team.

If you are summarizing the main points on this passage, you could maybe think it is not very easy to become a good leader. But only with this guide you cannot achieve being a leader like Larry Page, Steve Jobs or Bill Gates. On the one hand, they have unique qualities which are inimitable; on the other hand they can communicate their vision like no one else.

There are many different methods to communicate with your team, but essential for success is your individual way to communicate. Every person is different in his personality and needs a special handling.

With the right way of communication you can motivate your team endlessly. Communication gets a central role in leading a team. If you cannot transmit aims, measures, objectives and other relevant leadership methods correctly, you and your team will not be successful.

Larry Page managed it to communicate his leadership style to his members successfully. In the following part you will get some general information about his personality and his way of leading a team. His exceptional personality will be explained too.

Larry Page´s entrepreneur personality

In the topic "Classification of Larry Page´s leadership style" you got some information about Larry´s philosophy and his leadership style. In this case it was mentioned, that he is concentrating on three pillars, on which he is trusting. At first there is his special way of recruiting his employees. Important to know in this drop is his team orientated thinking. He developed his own individual application system, in which the applicants have to run through a professional interview, a phone call and eventually a phone call at Google office. Larry Page is searching for people, who have the right qualities for his projects. He needs people, who are sharing his idea of leading a team and his philosophy. Otherwise he cannot achieve success with his team. All in all he is searching for smart, talented and team orientated people with special qualities. He is not searching for experienced workers, but rather for people, who he can form after his idea. For him the nationality, the race or religion is not important to know, because he is open minded. That is why he can create a team after his agenda. One of his requirements is a high level of creativity to implement his vision. The second pillar of his way leading a team is motivation. On the way to success, he motivates every team member with financial or non-financial arguments. On the one side, he wants to support his team; on the other hand he prefers to build a relationship with his team. He believes that you only can work successfully in a good atmosphere. He is conferring his employees an extraordinary way of freedom at job. Larry Page trusts his team members, and that is the reason why an employee of Google gets so much freedom. On the other side, the employees of Google are appreciating Larry Page for his trust and work hardly to achieve common aims. Beside his qualities of leading, Larry Page has also special personal qualities, which are necessary for being successful. He has a clear vision and strategy for his team, he has the technical skills for giving advice or helping team members for developing their career, he is a good communicator and can also listen to the problems of his employees, and he can encourage his team. Many of these qualities are making the difference against normal leader. The basis of all activities of Page is his quality to communicate. He can transmit his vision perfectly to his team. In the theoretical part "leading a team successfully" you get to know, that you have to communicate aims, measures and objectives in the right way. You also need a special personality to achieve your employees. Larry Page for example, is a very introverted person. Introverts are the best leader for proactive employees. In the case of Google, where are mostly working proactive employees, a leader like Page has the ideal requirement of being successful. Introverted people are very good listener and not interested in dominating their team members. Furthermore Larry Page is a smart and lay back person, who thinks critically. He has a powerful passion and will, what is necessary to achieve personal and common aims. His greatest strength is his innovative thinking. On the basis of this, he created together with his team things, which changed the world.

All in all it is not only his leadership style, or his individual qualities, which make him to one of the best leader of this world. It is the entirety of all, which make him unique.

Conclusion

In the introduction of this paper, you get to know the differences between a manager and a leader. In the next topical, I specified some general information about Larry Page. After this, different styles of leadership were classified and explained. In the next step, I explained the leadership style of Larry Page and tried to classify it into one of the three I have listed before. Moreover I described his philosophy, the pillars of his leadership style, and his special qualities. At the end, the democratic leadership style and the one of Larry Page had the most conformity. In the next part, I explained what is necessary to lead a team successfully. Besides special qualities, you need good skills in communicating, motivating and recruiting. At the end it is a connection of all, what makes a good leader. After the theoretical part, Larry Page´s entrepreneur personality was mentioned. Here you get some information about the pillars of his success, his special qualities, and his personality.

At the end of this paper you will see, that Larry Page is one of the greatest leader of the world. There are many huge leader, but no one with such unique qualities. For Page it is not enough to lead a team successfully. He wants to build products, which will change the world. With his innovative thinking, his leadership qualities, his personality and philosophy, he has led Google to one of the most successful companies of the world. For this success, Page is searching for smart and young people with creative ideas. All of his employees are working for the mutual business goal. Page is an expert in recruiting, leading, motivating employees. Moreover he seeks the dialog with his team and verbalizes new requirements. Communication is very essential for him and also for his team. A good leader is very critical to him and tries to improve his abilities from time to time. When I have to describe Larry Page, I would say he is a smart person who is very introvert. He is a reserved person who respects his employees and this is the reason why his team respects him. If you summarize all of his leadership qualities and consider the success of Google and the satisfaction of his employees, you will also realize that Larry Page is one of the greatest leaders of the world. In my opinion you cannot compare Larry Page with other big leaders, because he lives with an autoimmune disease, which limits him in his life as well as in his job. Nevertheless his team respects him more as everybody else. Finally you have to think about his age. He is only 42 years old and has the possibility to improve himself in the next few years. Especially because he is so ambitious, we will see many new innovations of Google in the future. But despite the success of Google the principle "Don´t be evil" (Google Slogan) will hopefully be continued.

Literature review

Internet sources:

o   Educational-Business-Articles (2016): The leadership versus Management debate: What´s the difference?.http://www.educational-business-articles.com/leadership-versus-management/.(March 20th, 2016).

o   Academy of Achievement (2015): Larry Page Biography. Founding CEO, Googe Inc. http://www.achievement.org/autodoc/page/pag0bio-1.(March 22nd, 2016).

o   JENSEN, LYNDEN (2013): Laissez-Faire Leadership -Is Less More?. http://onhech.blogspot.de/2013/10/laissez-faire-leadership-is-less-more.html .(March 21st, 2016).

o   MARTIN, MARCI (2015): What Kind of Leader Are You? Traits, Skills and Styles. http://www.businessnewsdaily.com/2704-leadership.html.(March 20th,2016).

o   GILL, ERIC (2014a): What is Laissez-Faire Leadership? How Autonomy Can Drive Success. http://online.stu.edu/laissez-faire-leadership/.(March 20th, 2016).

o   GILL, ERIC (2014b): What is Autocratic Leadership? How Procedures Can Improve Efficiency. http://online.stu.edu/autocratic-leadership/.(March 20th, 2016).

o   GILL, ERIC (2014c): What is Democratic/Participative Leadership? How Collaboration Can Boost Morale. http://online.stu.edu/democratic-participative-leadership/.(March 20th, 2016).

o   CHERRY, KENDRA (2016): What Is Laissez-Faire Leadership? The Pros and Cons of the Delegative Leadership Style. http://psychology.about.com/od/leadership/f/laissez-faire-leadership.htm.(March 22nd, 2016).

o   GASTIL, JOHN (1994): A Definition and Illustration of Democratic Leadership. Article in "HUMAN RELATIONS" (Vol. 47, No 8, P. 953). https://www.researchgate.net/publication/247717389_A_Definition_and_Illustration_of_Democratic_Leadership.(March 23rd, 2016).

o   AKINYEMI, SEGUN (2014): Leadership Style. What Do People Do When They Are Leading . http://www.academia.edu/8094364/Leadership_Style.(March 21st, 2016).